Home Songs

Home Songs

SARAH REARDON

RESOURCE *Publications* • Eugene, Oregon

HOME SONGS

Resource Publications
An Imprint of Wipf and Stock Publishers
199 W. 8th Ave., Suite 3
Eugene, OR 97401

www.wipfandstock.com

PAPERBACK ISBN: 979-8-3852-4521-5
HARDCOVER ISBN: 979-8-3852-4522-2
EBOOK ISBN: 979-8-3852-4523-9
05/21/25

For Zachary, Esther, and those who are, LORD willing, to come.

CONTENTS

PREFACE

"These all died in faith, not having received the things promised, but having seen them and greeted them from afar, and having acknowledged that they were strangers and exiles on the earth. For people who speak thus make it clear that they are seeking a homeland ... they desire a better country, that is, a heavenly one. Therefore God is not ashamed to be called their God, for he has prepared for them a city."

—HEBREWS 11: 13-16

This book emanates from the conviction that home is a thing to be loved—both our current earthly homes and our ultimate heavenly home. Christian faith and Scripture lie beneath this conviction and the concomitant images and ideas expressed in these pages. While those familiar with Christianity and Scripture may perhaps be more likely to understand and appreciate these poems, the questions these poems together raise and the story they together tell should, I hope, be understandable to any reader.

The poems in this book all represent a pondering of the above passage and of the concept of "home." How ought an exile live well and make a home on this earth?

I do not believe that withdrawal from the good things of the world represents a good life for an exile. For God loves the world, and he has called it good. His "very good" design for the world is that men and women should not be alone but should live and flourish together, in families and communities.

Scripture gives a rich picture of the earthly home and family. The Psalmist describes the blessed life as one with children, who are compared to "olive shoots." The writers of Scripture consider barrenness a curse and children a gift. Throughout the book of Proverbs, Solomon presents wisdom as a Lady with a well-ordered, flourishing home. Solomon's book of love songs, too, portrays the beauty of a home hewn out of cedar, a wood which represents abundance and strength. The New Testament writers present a set of ethics for the household, and they command men to care for their households, living a "peaceful and quiet life" amid their homes. Paul commands Christians not to leave their given duties and places because of the new life Christ brings, but rather to serve all the more faithfully in their given places because of Christ. And Old Testament and New Testament writers alike consider earthly marriage as an image of the church's eternal union with God. All this suggests that Scripture honors the life of the earthly home.

A love of home—what philosopher Roger Scruton calls *oiko-philia*—resounds, too, throughout the great adventure stories of literary history.[1] In such stories, man returns to his place, and this return is the ground of the hero's joy. Hence the glory of home-coming in stories ranging from the ancient epics to famous fairy tales. Heroes often return to their rightful place after accomplishing great deeds—whether in Homer's *Odyssey*, with Odysseus's return to Ithaca, or in the tale of Jack and the Beanstalk, in which Jack returns to his family and restores to them their giant-snatched goods. In other stories, heroes re-establish their rightful place in a different form of homecoming—as in Virgil's *Aeneid*, with Virgil's re-creation of Troy in Rome, or the story of Cinderella, in which the virtuous maiden departs from a house of undue torment to her fitting place as a princess. The archetype of homecoming has historically resonated, across all varieties of literature, with joy and glory. And it finds its fullness in the Christian story: we, too, will return to the home we have known in part but not yet in full.

"Home," in short, should be a welcome word in our vocabulary. But how to make a home on earth and to love one's given

---

1. Scruton, *How to Think Seriously About the Planet*, 26.

place while also seeking "a better country, that is, a heavenly one"? To begin with, we must properly understand our station. As the Anglo-Catholic poet T.S. Eliot tells his reader in his *Four Quartets*, we are not "here to verify, instruct yourself, or carry report," but to kneel, and in such a position to find our rest.[2] We are not here on earth to succeed or promote ourselves, but to surrender ourselves. This is part of what it means to be a stranger and exile on the earth.

As with much of the Christian life and faith, homemaking as an exile is not an easy matter but a paradoxical pursuit. In considering such paradox Eliot's *Four Quartets* again comes to mind, particularly Eliot's charge at the end of "East Coker":

> We must be still and still moving
> Into another intensity
> For a further union, a deeper communion
> Through the dark cold and the empty desolation,
> The wave cry, the wind cry, the vast waters
> Of the petrel and the porpoise. In my end is my beginning.[3]

Such is the Christian life. It is a life of apparent contradiction: still and still moving, already and not yet. Loving our earthly homes and yet seeking a better one.

I have come to believe that homemaking here on earth is eschatological and profoundly spiritual. In marriage, in childbearing and rearing, in the ordinary life of caring for a place and contributing to a community—in these everyday things of the home we are picturing and practicing for eternity. To be faithful to God in the work of making a place here is indeed to seek "a better country," for to properly make and love a family and home on earth is to prepare for our heavenly homeland.

The poems in this book spring from the above conviction, and they dwell upon the home—broadly considered—and its truths and challenges and delights. You will not find many poems about "the kitchen" here, though it figures once or twice. I hope that these poems, written though they may be by a young

---

2. Eliot, *Four Quartets*, 46.
3. Eliot, *Four Quartets*, 29.

and inexperienced wife, mother, and homemaker, encourage you to consider in a new light the concept of home, along with all it contains and all it images.

ACKNOWLEDGEMENTS

Many thanks to the editors who published the following poems in their journals:

Ad Fontes Magazine: "Beneath the Cedar"

Modern Reformation: "Behold, He Comes"

Modern Age: "The Darkness of God"

Local Culture: "Around the Hearth" and "A Place Called Home"

Hearth and Field: "Ordinary Time" as "The Song of the Ordinary"

Amethyst Review: "Imperishable"

Wayfare: "Exiles on the Earth"

Home Songs

THE INTRODUCTION

Behold, cold rains have passed;
The winter speaks its last.
The time of singing comes;
The doves' low voices thrum.
The figs and vines burst forth,
And flowers cover earth.
Is this eternal spring?
What, then, might summer bring?
Impassable, this height,
Unrivaled joy, delight
Erupts from land and sky;
All creatures, glad, comply.
As if all shout, "Arise,
You must believe your eyes."
The calls of beauty say,
"Rise, dear one, come away."
A wedding feast awaits,
And these, though pearly, are but gates.
All this: a hint, a guess
To open what comes next.

BEHOLD, HE COMES

"The voice of my beloved! Behold, he comes,
leaping over the mountains, bounding over the hills."

—SONG OF SOLOMON 2:8

Besides the conversation of the cricket
And distant whirs of passing cars, no voice
Invades this night. The grazers in the thicket,
If not asleep, stay watching, stand with poise.
Unlike the doe, with soft eyes wide, content,
I watch with care as constant as a stoplight:
I flicker. Eyes soon droop, and spirit spent,
My ears benumbed to creatures out of sight.
But spoken words will shake me soon awake,
I know. I have been told. I will behold
The far-off voice, beloved, bound to break
This day with song and scatter all the cold
Of every quiet dusk. And when he comes
I will arise, my night of waiting gone.

BENEATH THE CEDAR

The ruddy trunk outlasts ten thousand trees,
Like cedar mid the winter's withered land.
Grown over years, a column made to stand,
And not to shiver with the passing breeze,
And not to sway wherever time decrees:
Such ones are rare within this dying land,
And hard to find. For I have searched and scanned:
The only tree of health, my eye now sees.

Indeed, like alabaster set on gold
He stands, and far and firm his boughs extend,
And under him I need not fear the cold.
But first I must acquire the heart to bend
Beneath his boughs, and from that place behold
The cedar's strength: yes, first, I must descend.

TO AENEAS, SEEKING A HOMELAND

I am the offered one, the promised prize
Of the battle you fight, of burning ships
And shifting loyalties and raging queens.
I am no shadow of your former wife,
But rather a woman of little luster,
Phoenician charm, or Trojan loveliness.
I am, however, the royal daughter:
The only child of the king and queen
Of Latium. A most-sought-after bride.
I'm not yet in my prime: I'm half your age,
A quarter (if that!) your experience.
I've sailed no seas and seen no shores but these,
I've fought no battles, nor seen battles fought
Over my hand or land—besides this one,
The war you wage against our settled place.

And so I write to you, because I've seen
My mother's crazed eyes, darkened countenance,
And heard her muttered hatred for my father.
I've seen the slaves with guilty face discuss
The rumors lacing Latium, as flame
Unravels through the wood and climbs each tree
Until it crests the forest's crown of leaves.
I've heard you left your burning home in Troy—

Obediently left the war for peace—
To bear your gods and line to restoration,
To bring a glorious race to recreation.
Yes, stories lick our streets in crackling blaze,
Just as the omen crackled at the altar:
The burning hair that scattered light divine,
And scared us all, and sealed, it seems, my glory.

These things confirm your words: that you have come,
As you have promised, to take us and raise
Toward the stars the little Latin people.
Though bitter with the taste of battled days,
You will bring peace through war, as we believe.
Oh pious one, you must press onward, trust
That home is found here, not just forged of will.
This is a place to rest, not simply rule.
Our land is rich with olive, cypress, laurel,
And many gentle hills of matching color;
Our people, brave and sometimes kind. You'll find
Amidst this place—in me—a willing wife
Not practiced, passionate, or puffed with beauty
But patient, seeking after piety.
The Latins may be stubborn, clinging swords,
But I will only hold an open hand.
Here seek, here find—this, your promised homeland.

THE WEDDING

These two at altar body forth our end:
The world will wed before her time to mend.
We wait, as she was patient for her groom,
A ceremony of great joy and doom.

EARLY DAYS

Such are the days of our beginning: brief,
But laced with novelty like morning light,
Which graces half-drawn shades and bleary eyes.
Before we stumble where the dawn invites,
We tarry, smiling, over toast and coffee,
Then linger over prayer before we break
To go our ways and wait the night's return:
To come home to this place we did not make.

These days will end; with them, our energy.
Someday we will not rush to greet, to kiss,
Someday returning will be commonplace,
Without the rush of first affection's bliss.
But under heaven, each receives a season.
These early days are ours—to clasp and hold,
To taste and savor morning's honeyed light,
To learn what does, and what does not, grow old.

HOME SONG

We fill the empty room
With nothing but a stool.
The room then grows a gloom
Because it is not full.

We lack but one knick-knack
To decorate the place.
We talk about our lack
And sip the gloom of space.

We almost long for junk
To rid the empty room
Of that which makes us drunk:
This draught of barren gloom.

Yet as our stupor wanes,
I start to see a light
That comes not through the panes:
A ray from out of sight.

And in the ray unseen
I glimpse a future mirth
That makes the barren green
And gives this room a hearth.

The stool could sit a man
Who strums and sings and leads
His chorus, round him fanned,
In ancient hymns and creeds.

The little ones would dance,
And pull him down to play.
His wife will join the dance
And draw the man away.

In years, these very floors
Will rumble rich with feet:
We'll open wide our doors
And guests anew will meet,

And round our table, feast,
With growing olive shoots
Who bring the scent of peace
And glory to their roots.

The room, for now, is still
Arrayed with just a stool.
But now I see it will
By grace, in time, be full.

THE DARKNESS OF GOD

After T.S. Eliot[1]

Not here the darkness, in this twittering world,
But there, perhaps, in solitude, unseeing,
The child in temporary comfort curled—
A darkness known by this half-knowing being.
Though further still he will descend, he stirs
Or rests, for now, within this *world not world,*
The world within the world, the womb that whirs
With whispered words—his name, like him, still furled.
This is the only way. And yet it's dear:
Both known and hidden in this deepest shade,
Both formed and forming yet, with none to fear,
Yet fearfully and wonderfully made.
Dependent on another's bread and breath—
Beloved, this is the way of birth and death.

---

1. Selections in italics from Eliot, *Four Quartets,* 15.

TO A PROMISED ONE

The summer has ended, harvest passes, yet
We are not saved. When will redemption come?
When will this waiting cease? We only guess.
I sense the air has changed: it tastes of hay.
And days have shed their color as we wander,
Just as the wind, with bitter spirits, roves:
It seeks from east to west yet finds no rest.

Beside the road, the leaves begin to blow.
We watch, awaiting winter's coming,
Like children gathering brush, collecting scraps,
We scramble to assemble what we need
For your arrival from a distant country—
A place perhaps not far but hard to find,
A province ever hidden from our eyes.

Dear one, for now you cannot see the fall
In all its burning hues and swirling gusts,
Its stinging air, its scent of death, half-sweet.
But you will feel its bite before you cry,
You'll sense the fall behind your still-closed eyes.
And maybe even now you know its chill—
That this is not a green world—if a garden,
Then tangled, shriveled, full of rotting trees.

What sudden spring could rain upon such land?
What chance of foretold fruit, the rebirth vowed?
Some light our wary eyes have not yet seen.
We wonder how the promise will play out—
What does it mean that you are set apart?
You grow like every other child, you kick
And glide around, exploring home—the womb,
Which shelters you in darkness and pains me.

We wait and we prepare. You move; we smile
But do not feel the joy, not yet. Until
Our hands can touch and eyes can see the one
We have anticipated, half-believed,
Our hope is hazy as the autumn mist.
And yet, as on November mornings, ample.
For mist unravels into every glade
And spreads its fingers over every field.
It dresses all in white; it washes all,
With water beads bejeweling everything.
Our hope exalts this waiting, makes it holy.

HANNAH'S HOLIDAY

Her hands are quick with knowledge as she weaves
Upon the robe its final vibrant strands.
Her fingers quake, just momentarily,
Then brush her face, and with resolve, she stands,
Begins preparing for the yearly journey:
The bread her hands have made, he never eats,
The crops his family grows, he never sees,
The crowd of brothers whom he never meets.
"Not mine, O LORD, but yours," she prays,
As others have, and will, with tears and sweat.
And Hannah, being feeble, binds on strength
And climbs the temple steps, her face still wet
But heart exulting and mouth wide with joy.
The LORD kills and brings to life—all at once.
She rushes now to meet her little boy,
She looks to him as joyous as if drunk.

RACHEL'S CHILDREN

Around the corner, roses grow
Beneath a wall with green arrayed.
A tree its foreground graces, lone,
Its branches giving fruit and shade.

And by it flows a stream of blue.
All this, above the flower tops,
Bejeweled with buds and bees and dew,
Just steps away from where we stop.

Upon the dirtied curb we stand
And bow our heads, or speak, or weep
At what the entrants here have planned
For budding lives they will not keep.

One crosses now from car to gate:
Gaze downward, fixed upon her walk,
Her shoes in an impoverished state;
Her trembling hands reveal her thoughts.

Another exits as she comes,
Her head held high: the hardened nurse,
Whose hands are used to drawing blood,
Now lights a smoke and sounds a curse

When reading something on her phone.
For us, she, too, averts her eyes.
Her face assumes its look of stone:
Conviction dead, or well-disguised.

A car drops off, then darts away.
Its brazen woman flips the bird
At what the Christians have to say.
Amidst the spat, a voice unheard:

Not that of swearing passersby,
Or bikers spitting in disgust,
And not the vested escorts' lies,
And not the pleas proclaimed by us.

But somewhere deep in time, a cry,
Lamenting for the lives she's lost
To this most ancient form of crime,
The death we've claimed as freedom's cost.

While Rachel cries and clamor reigns,
For all the edicts Herod gives,
The verdant grass and streams remain.
The garden round the corner lives.

AN INVITATION

To find the one who leaves the ninety-nine
Is not to follow in your father's line
But is to enter narrow doors and dine
On bread and drink that ninety-nine decline.

AROUND THE HEARTH

We traded tales of stars upon the meadows
From days before the sky was colored grey
Around the roughened oaken tabletop
And round the reddening flame that autumn day.
Our time then burned till sleep inflamed our eyes.

The tales were more than talk, but light in the dark,
Each story an illuminating ray.
And only after lingering long, we left,
Each one to bed to dream of bygone days
Before another dawn brought work again.

How good it is to cease at dusk, withdraw,
And circle round the hearth with drink and bread
And stay up late to tell, or hear, of time:
Its common glories, troughs and peaks, are tread
By roving souls, aglow with common grace.

ORDINARY TIME

As signs of supper shared await
The daily scrub and sweep of crumbs,
The kitchen croons of its estate:
It works. It welcomes, warms, then sends.
Meanwhile, the dough in patience grows.
The children chatter, bicker, laugh,
The faucet drips, the fan still blows,
As footsteps patter in and pause.
No feast but Sunday's to prepare,
Her hands, with rhythm, stir the soup.
Through open windows wafts cool air,
Resounding with late morning song:
The birds, resuming work, are shrewd.
They chirp of ordinary days—
Of keeping nests, of finding food—
And flit from branch to branch, at peace.

DOWNTOWN

Returning home, we travel into town,
Where ever-various faces gaze on bricks
That never change, and eager tourists wait
For fudge not quite homemade but loved well here.
We've known and loved this place through sun and rain.
Despite the flags they hang, or slogans claimed,
An almost sacred something dwells downtown.

We cross the bridge and watch the passing boats.
We walk the dock and dance along the edge.
We sit beneath magnolias long beloved,
And in the bayside sun admire the blooms
For what they, too, become: an open door,
A lighthouse beacon beckoning back to land,
A highway sign with bright words pointing home.

A PLACE CALLED HOME

"The LORD of hosts has sworn in my hearing: 'Surely many
houses shall be desolate, large and beautiful houses, without
inhabitant.'"

—ISAIAH 5:9

One weekday morn I strolled
Beneath suburban trees and wires,
Past porches silent, cold,
Like chimneys long unused to fire.

What good is it to own
A dwelling place where no one dwells?
Who loves a vacant home,
The kind that quickly sells—

Pristine, unpeopled rooms,
And well-made beds and tidy floors,
Where deathless shadows loom,
Or sunlight, unseen, unknown, pours?

Come morning, tenants leave—
Still eating, rush from door to car,
With lunches packed, shirts cleaned,
And no desire for where they are.

They only seek the next
Occupation—destination—
A journey without rest.
Their homes stand still, always patient.

Not so for me. I stride
Toward familiar trees that wave
To welcome me inside
A door well loved; a home well named.

CAIN AND ABEL, IN YOUTH

"The LORD said to Cain, 'Why are you angry, and why has your
face fallen? If you do well, will you not be accepted? And if you
do not do well, sin is crouching at the door. Its desire is for you,
and you must rule over it.'"

—GENESIS 4:6-7

What innocence is pictured here:
The brothers toddle round the hearth.
They chase each other without fear,
And Father, sitting by, just smiles.
The older, gentle, turns around
To let his brother tackle him.
In play, they fall upon the ground.
Their fight resounds with laughter.

Who will remember this in years?
When shouting starts and fills the house
And Mother's watching eyes with tears;
When anger springs upon the door,
Upon the brother, gentle once,
Who will be cheered by memory?
The crouching thing gets what it wants:
The predator to innocence

Is also enemy of joy,
Forgetfulness's closest friend:
The toddling, laughing little boy,
His brother, sweet, his mom and dad—
They all forget the way they were,
The moment's lost to time.
Their youth, by pain, becomes a blur
Beneath a damning stroke of red.

And thus an exile is made.
And thus a sinner gets his due.
The home destroyed, the brother slain—
A curse has rightly been declared.
As Cain wanders, his sorrow grows.
Like him, we settle east of Eden,
But still, we bear a mark that shows
That God has not forgotten.

FATHERS AND DAUGHTERS

I see him now: he crouches mid the grass,
Which stands uncut, arrayed with dew. He talks,
Converses, coaxes midst his gardening tasks,
While weeding, whispers to raspberry stalks.
"You must grow," says he, yet in sweeter words.
Like him, his words remain unknown, but guessed,
Imagined with the aid of all I've heard,
And pondered, often, for their tenderness.

I see his son. He waits beside the river,
Which ripples, radiant with dawn. He sings,
With soft tones serenades his hoped-for dinner
And waits to take what treasures time will bring.
"You reel in slow," he tells his watching child,
"But jerk the tip up quick if something bites."
I stood there, mystified, and meekly smiled,
And drank it in—the humming morning light.

I see that time, like berries, ripens red,
Is plucked and shared and savored while it lasts.
The years, like fish, are caught, and we are fed.
But only after a slow reel, well cast.
For from my father and his father,
Always the lesson, learned or not, was patience.

May we, too, teach this to our daughter,
And, like our fathers, sing within our station.

IMPERISHABLE

To "Baba" Julie Soltis

All life is vapor, as are our life stories.
All flesh is grass, and so are all its glories.
But there is yet a time to watch the mists,
To search the grass for beauty that persists:
For glints of that which does not fade or wither,
Cannot be bought and worn like gold and silver.
A sight which hints, instead, of things unfading:
Along the shore, a woman wending, wading,
She bends to gather shells she'll stow away
Collected to give to someone someday.
Or round the mountaintop, she gathers flowers
And greets a stranger, stops to talk for hours,
Returns home late, and stoops to prayer, not rest,
Refreshed by well-worn paths that guide the blessed.
A gentle spirit, with an open door,
Who gives the tea and bread she has, and more,
She gives an answer for her hope with glee,
That joy that lasts until eternity.

EXILES ON THE EARTH

"No place is permanent," the gravestones sing,
"And even we return unto the dust."
But we who pass the stones forget these things,
The grave and what it has to do with us.
We move in circles—work, park, market, gym,
Perhaps the neighbor's house, perhaps the church.
We circle, tireless, till our soles grow thin,
And only then might we begin to search
For permanence of which all dust has dreamed,
Which graveyards, undisturbed, have not yet known:
A city, strong as cedar and as green,
For fairer country, higher ground, or home.
To those who circle not, but bend their knees—
Theirs is the better land, the mountain breeze.

BIBLIOGRAPHY

Eliot, T.S. *Four Quartets*. London: Faber & Faber, 2019.
Scruton, Roger. *How to Think Seriously About the Planet: The Case For An Environmental Conservatism*. Oxford: Oxford University Press, 2012.